Guided Self Healing Meditations

Mindfulness Meditation Including Anxiety and Stress Relief Scripts, Chakras Healing, Meditation for Deep Sleep, Panic Attacks, Breathing and More.

By Healing Meditation Academy

"Guided Self Healing Meditations: Mindfulness Meditation Including Anxiety and Stress Relief Scripts, Chakras Healing, Meditation for Deep Sleep, Panic Attacks, Breathing and More." Written by "Healing Meditation Academy".

Guided Self Healing Meditations is a bundle of the books "Guided Meditations for Mindfulness and Self Healing", & "Guided Self-Healing and Mindfulness Meditations Bundle".

Hope You Enjoy!

Guided Meditations for Mindfulness and Self Healing

Follow Beginners Meditation Scripts for Anxiety and Stress Relief, Deep Sleep, Panic Attacks, Depression, Relaxation and More for a Happier Life!

By Healing Meditation Academy

Table of Contents

Guided Meditations for Mindfulness and Self Healing
Chapter 1: Mindfulness Meditation

Beginner Breathing (10 minutes if done individually)

The Stimulating Breath: The aim here is to enhance your overall alertness and internal energy sources.
The 4-7-8 Exercise

Breathing Exercise Three:

Breathe Counting
Anger Relaxation
Grief Relaxation

Chapter 2: Chakra Healing Meditation

Root Chakra Meditation (Meditation time approx. 15 when repeated 2 times)

Root (2)

Sacral Chakra Meditation (Meditation time approx. 15 when repeated 2 times)

Sacral Chakra (2)

Solar Plexus Meditation (Meditation time approx. 15 when repeated 3 times)

Solar Plexus (2)

Heart Chakra Meditation (Meditation time approx. 15 when repeated 2 times)

    Heart (2)

Throat Chakra Meditation (Meditation time approx. 15 when repeated 3 times)

    Throat (2)

Third Eye Chakra Meditation (Meditation time approx. 15 when repeated 2 times)

    Third eye (2)

Crown Chakra Meditation (Meditation time approx. 10 when repeated 3 times)

    Body Scan (10 mins. Repeat 5x)

Chapter 1: Mindfulness Meditation

Beginner Breathing (10 minutes if done individually)

The Stimulating Breath: The aim here is to enhance your overall alertness and internal energy sources.

- Begin by first inhaling and then exhaling in a rapid manner through your nostrils. Remember to keep your mouth completely closed but still very relaxed. Ensure that your breathing is exactly equal in its duration while making sure that the breaths are short. You will find that this particular exercise is rather loud.

- Aim for around 3 inhales and exhales each second. This will create a very sharp movement of your diaphragm— similar to a bellows. After each individual breathing cycle, you can start to breathe normally for a short period of around 1 minute.

- On your very first attempt, refrain from doing this for more than 20 seconds. You can, however, increase your time by the duration of 5 seconds until a full minute has been reached. After a while of performing this exercise, you will likely feel boosts of energy and awareness similar to a great workout.

The 4-7-8 Exercise

Begin by sitting with your back completely straight. Then, place this tip of the tongue along with the tissue that sits right behind the upper portion of your front teeth— hold it here for the duration of the exercise. This exercise will require that you exhale through your mouth and around the tongue. If the movement is too awkward, you can also purse your lips for added comfort.

- Exhale all the way through your mouth, creating a whooshing noise.

- Next, inhale silently after closing your mouth. Inhale through your nose for a total duration of 4 seconds.

- Ensure that your breath is held for a period of 7 seconds.

- Now, begin to exhale with a whooshing noise through your mouth for 8 seconds.

- This counts as one cycle of breathing. Now, you are to inhale once again and restart the original cycle. Do this 3 times totaling 4 breaths.
Keeping mind that this breathing excursive requires that you

continually inhale through the nose and exhale through the mouth. Make sure that your tongue is kept in the same position at all times during the exercise. Also, you will notice that exhaling will last nearly twice the amount of time as inhaling will. However, the total amount of time that is spent during each breathing sessions is not of integral importance just as long as you remember the 4:7:8 ratios.

Breathing Exercise Three:

Breathe Counting

Perform this meditative exercise for 10-15 minutes per session. This time is preferred because it allows you to fully garner all of the best benefits that mindfulness meditation has to offer. However, if you are pressed for time, you will find that even a few minutes will carry many benefits for you as well.

- Sit in a comfortable position with your back completely straight and your head leaning forward.

- Start to shut your eyes and inhale slowly and deeply.

- Next, exhale slowly without being too forceful. You want this rhythm to be slow and quiet, but it is okay if these vary for you.

- Acknowledge incoming thoughts even if they are plentiful. Let go of them and return to your breath as soon as you recognize that you have become distracted.

- Start conducting a full scan of your body from the top of your head down to your feet.

- Notice any subtle or strong sensations in all of the areas that you scan.

- As you move along your body and begin to notice sensations, recognize them and let go. The goal is only to heighten awareness of these sensations, rather than trying to change them.

- Now, count "one" when you exhale. Remember to release your breath very slowly and at a measured pace.

- Next, count "two"... continues sequentially to a count of five totals.

- Once you have reached a count of five, restart the cycle by counting "one" for the next exhale.

- Be sure to refrain from counting any higher than 5 once you exhale. If your count reaches beyond 5, this is a clear indication of your attention having wondered.

In this next module for mindfulness meditation, we will tackle pain management. I will guide you along with a session designed to have you concentrate on acceptance and observation. In this way, you will be able to morph all of your pain, and then focus your mind during the meditation exercise to install both mental and physical calm and relief from pain.

– So, start by finding and settling into a comfortable position ensuring that your back has enough support. While you are laying on your back, or if you are seated in a chair with enough support for your head, you can begin this session.

- As you come to settle yourself, take notice of how your body and mind feel in this unique moment. Remember, you do not need to attempt to change anything at this moment. Simply become a patient, calm and distant observer of your physical and mental state. Managing pain starts with simple and calm observation.

- Now, notice where some of your pain and tension is being carried. Where is the pain in your body? Which parts of your body are calm and at ease?

- Start conducting a full scan of your body from the top of your head down to your feet.

- Notice any subtle or strong sensations in all of the areas that you scan.
- As you move along your body and begin to notice sensations, recognize them and let go. The goal is only to heighten awareness of these sensations, rather than trying to change them.
- Take another deep inhaling breath... then release your breath through a calm and slow exhale.

- Breath in again....now breath out.

- Keep breathing... slowly... calmly.

- Now, conduct another scan of your body:

Feel the soles of your feet on the floor

Feel the cold air inhaled through your nostrils

Notice any unique bodily sensations that you are feeling

When you are distracted or lost in thought, bring your attention right back to your breath

Feel the rise and fall of your chest as you inhale and exhale

Feel and notice where the movement of your breath is felt in your body

Notice the influx of thoughts and then return to a bodily sensation or the breath

Notice where your body is uneasy or uncomfortable

Notice whether your breaths are shallow or deep without changing them

Feel the cold air moving through your nostrils and filling your chest causing it to expand.

Let go of any pain that you feel move along your body. Do not judge your pain or sensations, whether they are positive or negative, just be at peace and passive accept them.

Anger Relaxation

– Start by finding and settling into a comfortable position ensuring that your back has enough support. While you are laying on your back, or if you are seated in a chair with enough support for your head, you can begin this session.

- Where is your tension being held in your body?
- Where, if anywhere, is the pain located in your body?
- Is any part of your body totally relaxed?
- Now, perform a full body scan from the top of your head to the soles of your feet.
- Breath in... and breath out now.
- Focus on your breath, bringing its rhythm to a smooth flow in and out of your mouth with no rush.
- Now, keep going onward with the

management of your pain through relaxation breathing. There is no need to force anything to take place; just notice how your body is feeling, without judgment, or negativity. If you begin to have negative thoughts and feelings, bring your focus right back to your breath. Just passively observe.

- Keep observing the state of your discomfort and pain-free from judgment. Your body is constantly changing, feeling one way at one moment, and another the next.

- This moment to moment state of change is constant. Simply observe each and every moment as it comes and passes ever so peacefully.

- While all of our pain is not wanted

and hard to cope with, try to focus on your pain with an aura of acceptance and peace. Free from judgment and pain.

Accept and be at peace with how you feel emotionally and physically. Resistance is the cause of suffering and discomfort.
- Accepting and observing are key to moving beyond your pain and anger, and allowing yourself to step into peace and acceptance.
- Focus on simply allowing your body, mind, and spirit to just... be. Be still and at total ease— whether you feel positively or negatively.
- Repeat. I totally accept all of myself. I love who I am.
- I fully accept the pain that I am

feeling.
- I completely release the need that I have for control over how I feel and judgment for the way that I feel.
- I accept all aspects of who I am with love and peace ... free of pain and judgment.
- When distracted bring all of your focus directly back to your breath once again.

When you feel ready, bring all of your attention to the sounds of your surroundings... slowly; when you are ready... open your eyes. Refreshed and awakened, you are free to move through your day at ease and peace.

Grief Relaxation

Relax in a comfortable position. You can be seated or on the floor. Whichever bests suits you at the present moment. Just be... Allow your thoughts, however urgent and furious they enter your mind, to simply pass through your mind with calmness and acceptance.

Focus on your breath, bringing in the deep, cool air that fills your lungs. Now, exhale slowly and peacefully. Do this 3 more times; each time bring all of your focus to your breath calmly and with ease. Fully immerse yourself into this present moment of calm and wellness.

Now, begin observing your present thoughts. Notice any particular thoughts about your pain and grief. Are there thoughts of loss? Do you feel as though you want to change these thoughts? Fight against the temptation to change these thoughts. Simply allows them to flow into your mind, and simply label them as "grief" or "loss" or "pain."

Notice that when you simply label these thoughts, there is a sudden distance that you have created from them. Indeed, these are not who you truly are. They are just ephemeral thoughts.

After labeling these thoughts, bring

your attention back to your breath once again. Inhaling and exhaling with calm ease. Notice the coolness of the air coming into your nostrils and leaving out of your mouth.

Now, focus on the areas of discomfort in your body. Imagine an altered sensation; this can be whichever sensation or feeling that you choose to experience. You might also want to feel a nice tingle along your leg or forearm. This will give you added control over your physical sensations, even if just for a fleeting moment.

Now, feel this sensation in full. Feel it replacing your feelings and thoughts of having lost somebody or something. Allow this sensation to replace your pain and grief. More and more, one bit at a time, allow your grief to go away.

This sensation will allow you to relax and let go of your grief. This distance is healthy and peaceful for you. Now, take a deep inhale... now breath out. In and out... once again... in and out. The cool air is a calming sensation for your body, mind, and spirit.

Embrace the energy of passively accepting your feelings and thoughts. Simply allow yourself to fully embrace how you are feeling and whichever emotional, mental and physical state that you are in at this present moment.

Breath in calmly and slowly; inhaling and exhaling. Allow yourself to be an observer of every breath and let your breathing be deep and peaceful. Embrace calmness and wholeness with each and every one of your breaths.

Be aware of all that your senses perceive at the present moment in time. Focus on one thought at a time, and label them.

Notice each sound that comes to your ears. Feel how your clothes sit on your body again. Just observe without feeling as though you have to change something.

Now, in closing, scan your body from the top of your head to the soles of your feet. Allow all of your physical sensations along the way to be fully embraced without judgment or a need to change them. Peacefully move along your body.
When you have reached your feet, bring your attention to your breath one last time. Inhale and exhale slowly and peacefully... when you are ready...

Open your eyes.

Chapter 2: Chakra Healing Meditation

Root Chakra Meditation (Meditation time approx. 15 when repeated 2 times)

Officially, the name of the first chakra is actually, Muladhara, and is derived from two words: Mula, meaning root, and Dhara— meaning support. The main role of this particular chakra is to connect the entirety of your energy with that of the Earth. This exercise is called grounding. When considering the Root Chakra, you should consider this as day-to-day survival on earth.

Moreover, the central role of this energy is to provide you with all that you need to survive and live a fruitful life here on earth. In today's current society and time period, this idea tends to manifest as emotional as well as financial security.

Now...

Be comfortable. If your body is lying on the floor, allow your entire body to relax and feel comfortable fully. If sitting, allow your hands to be relaxed on your thighs or just resting on our side. Either posture is fine.

Now, shut your eyes. This time is perfectly laid out for you. Let all of your anxieties go. Let your spirit flow beautifully into the present moment. This current moment is all that exists; there is no past, no future; neither exists. Only the present moment is here now.

Let your shoulders rest and drop. Allow your hands to rest completely. Let your body, in its full form, become soft and settle naturally. Let your face be fully calm, as well as your eyes, and hair. Unclench your jaw and allow your body's muscles to ease fully. Become soft.

Take in a clean breath; this will cleanse your spirit and allow you to relax. Let go of all of the tension in your body. Let your breathing to settle with a natural motion naturally. Resist the temptation to control your breath. Just be an observer of your breath, thoughts, and emotions. Breath in, breath out; observe the rhythm of the breath. Just observe.

Now, bring your mind's attentiveness and energy to the spine's base. Visualize a small red light, swirling in a circle, almost like a small whirlpool. Just observe and notice how it feels and looks. Acquire a keen sense of how your breath is functioning. What speed is the breath? Is it accelerated or is it slower? Breathe in and breathe out all of the tension within your body and spirit. Now breathe the red light into your body. Feel this air in the Base Chakra. Observe the red light filling the Base Chakra and spreading outwardly. Breathe in while attracting the red light closer to you. Feel the warmth of this red light. Breathe in and breathe out the tension. Slowly repeat without judgment but as an observer.

The red light attracts with it health, strength and a strong sense of security. When this red light fills you, allow it to spread to your feet, feel the empowerment that the light brings as it fully connects with the energy of the earth. Feel the calm and relaxing energy of the red light. Breathe in the earth's fresh and calming energy.

Breath into your body personal security, self-confidence, and breath out ever fear within your spirit. Remind yourself that you are fully safe, secure and in touch with your spirit.

Now it is time to close this chakra. Bring all of your attention to the small red light that rests at the Base Chakra. Visualize this light becoming smaller, bringing it all the way down to the size of a thimble. Now, begin the mantra, The Base Chakra is functioning with complete normality." "My spirit now has an approach to my earthly needs that is balanced and calm. Every single need of mine is fully cared for."

Bring all of your awareness to the incoming and outgoing flow of the breath. Breathe in and breathe out. Feel the cool breathing as it enters your nostrils and flows all the way down to the back of the throat and all the way into the full expansion of your lungs. Be aware of the natural movement of the stomach as it expands and contracts. Feel your body resting against the floor. Feel your fingers, shrug the shoulders. When you are completely ready, calmly open your eyes.

Root (2)

Take a long, drawn out deep breath. When you exhale, adjust your attention to your spinal base. Now, visualize a red chakra that is shining brightly. The warmth and glow of this chakra relaxes your mind and heart, allowing you to fully feel the safety and serenity that this chakra brings.

Feel grounded and unshaken as if you are a massive rock that is held warmly by the earth. Visualize yourself standing calmly at the base of a snowy mountain that is lifting itself upward toward the sky. Right in front of you is a massive opening that leads to a cave. The suns's rays enter in an inviting way as you walk into the cave.

Take a step forward and walk inside the cave. You will see that the cave is surrounded by smooth walls and a ceiling that extends very high. There is a warm, soft and gentle breeze that allows you to feel comfortable. Walk a little farther and be aware of your surroundings.

You now notice a path that has opened into a big, circular room. There is a large rectangular rock sitting in the middle. A small and warm ray of sun is slipping through a tiny fissure in the ceiling and bathes the stone with a glow of warmth.

Walk over to the rock and take a seat on it. Sit cross-legged- this will come naturally to you.

You now start to feel as though you are an appendage of the mountain- as though you are a piece of it. You feel anchored very deeply connected to the earth. You are safe. You can see that the earth is nourishing and supporting every aspect of your being.

Now you can see that your first chakra is spinning and beginning to gain strength. As this chakra starts to spin much faster, a red light spans over you and enters every single feel in your body, and even every pore.

Allow the calm from your surrounding see into your body and spirit, enhancing your peace and inner serenity.

Take a deep breath and allow yourself to feel the energy that has funnelled to the bottom of your spine. Hold onto this feeling of high energy for an extended period, becoming filled with good energy and peace. Now, once your feel filled with the great energy of this state, let go of this feeling and focus your attention on your breath, breathing in slowly and exhaling in the same way.

Relax within this state of awareness. This awareness will lead you toward your very best self. You are stronger, calmer and more peaceful than ever before.

Now, rise in a gentle manner, and walk out of the room, through the path to the outside of the cave. Take a gaze back at the mountain and feel connected to it— as though you are one with it.

Once you are ready, you can open your eyes and rise.

Sacral Chakra Meditation (Meditation time approx. 15 when repeated 2 times)

This second chakra knows as the sacral chakra or svadhishana translates directly to "the place of the self." Notably, this chakra is most concerned with one's identity as a human being and how one is to deal with it. Perhaps the most beneficial aspect of this chakra is that it provides one with creative energy to maximize their enjoyment of life.

Get yourself into a comfortable position. If you are laying on the floor, allow your entire body to fully relax and become comfortable. If you are sitting in a chair, settle your hands on your thighs or at the side of your body.

Now, close your eyes. This time if uniquely set out for you. Leave all of your worries. Let them go.

Have awareness for all of the sounds that surround you; just allow them to be present without judgment or interaction.

Be aware of the shade and light permeating through your eyelids. Feel the soft cool air softly touching your body's surface.

Sense the massive sky above you, along with the broad horizons that stretch around you, feel the earth below you, supporting your weight and body.

Draw in a breath that cleanses you and then breath out all of the tension that has built up inside of your body and mind. Let your breath fall naturally into a rhythm.

When your thoughts arise and begin to distract you, just gently bring your attention back to your breath. Breathe in and breathe out with awareness.

Now, draw your attention to your abdomen. Visualize a beautiful orange light that is swirling in a way that is similar to a small pool. Be aware of how this feels, what does it look like? What is the function of this light? Is there a tingling feeling? Gently notice the thoughts in your mind, how fast are they? Are they troubling you? Can you visualize the orange color within your mind?

Bring your attention back to your breath now. Breathe in calm, breath out resistance and tension. Now breathe into yourself the orange light of warm. Notice how this light is breathed into your abdomen area—directly into your Sacral Chakra. Allow this energy to spread outward to your surroundings, sending love and positivity.

Kindly welcome all of the pleasureful dealings that this orange light brings. Breath in joy and breath out all of the tension inside of you (Repeat in rhythm).

Now, it is time to close this chakra down. Bring all of your attention to your abdomen, to the orange light of the Sacral Chakra. Notice this light getting smaller, all the way down to the small size of a fairy's light. Bring this light into normal function. Repeat the mantra, "My Sacral Chakra has begun operating normally."

Draw your awareness to the soft, cool flow of your breath. Breathe in and out in a repeated rhythm. Be aware of the cool air as it enters your nostrils and down the throat, filling your lungs fully. Let yourself notice the natural and soft motion of your stomach when you inhale and exhale. Rest in awareness as your entire body is resting against the floor, or in your chair. Bring all of your attention to your hands and move them slowly. Feel the physical sensation of this motion. Shrug your shoulders and drop them slowly if they are tense. Feel the temperature of the room, and hear all of the sounds that are nearby.

When you are fully ready, open your eyes and rise slowly.

Sacral Chakra (2)

Get into a comfortable position. Either on the floor or seated gently in a chair. Your hands in your lap and feet on the floor.

Notice your physical sensations, followed by resting in awareness of the sounds around you and the temperature in the room that you are in.

Now, invite in the orange color of the setting sun. Allow yourself to be encompassed by your Hara, with orange light being the source of empowerment, balance, and motivation. Feed your Hara and repeat the mantra, "I will honor all of my sacred personal needs." "I hereby will allow my spirit to be fully nourished."

When you are ready, adjust your awareness to the gents and the soft region just below your breast bone. This area is your Solar Plexus; this is the chakra of personal power.

Now, begin to breathe in, and allow your solar plexus to become soft and gently expand your breath. Allow an orange light to wash over you now, providing warmth and comfort, feeling your personal power and self-belief.

Breathe in the refreshing energy that comes with this self-belief. Breathe into your Sacral Chakra- the source of your personal power. Feel this empowered, motivated and strengthened energy. Notice your thoughts without judgment, are they more empowered? Do you feel stronger mentally? Rest in awareness of these thoughts without judging them or feeling the need to change them in any way.

Breath in and breath out, repeat in rhythm and harmony of the movement in your belly. Feel the expansion of your body as you breathe in and breathe out.

Welcome all pleasing feelings and thoughts without judgment, but appreciation for them. Allow them to energize you as you continue the rhythm of your breath.

Allow the orange light to cover and encompass you now. Feel the warmth of this light.

Rest in this awareness as you continue breathing in and out, in the rhythm of calm and relaxation hue noticing your personal power through the Sacral Chakra.

Feel the physical sensations of your body now. Your feet on the floor, your hands in your lap. When you are ready, open your eyes and arise.

Solar Plexus Meditation (Meditation time approx. 15 when repeated 3 times)

This chakra directly translates to, "lustrous gem." Interestingly, this is the chakra from which your self-belief, confidence and personal power are bred. If you have been a circumstance that was not right for you, or, conversely, a situation where you had a gut feeling that things were going to work out— then you have tapped into the Solar Plexus chakra. Truly, this is your personal power, or solar plexus, at work. You can feel this confidence in physical form within your body, or "gut."

Sit on the edge of a cushion or soft blanket. Form a fist with your right hand and make a cup with your left hand. Now, extend the thumb on your right hand upward. Place the right fist within your open left palm, draw each of your hands right in front of your solar plexus; this is located just elbow your sternum and right above the navel cavity.

Now, close your eyes and connect in a synchronized manner with the rising and falling of your breath.

Imagine that a flame has replaced your right thumb. This flame flickers at the center of your entire being. With every inhale that you initiate, watch this yellow flame grow bigger and brighter. Visualize and feel the warmth that spreads from this region of your body and fills you first from the inside, and outwardly from you. Next, imagine that you've grabbed a small group of sticks. On each and every stick, you will write down a phrase or just a word that represents something within your life that is no longer of service to you. This can be something that you are in the midst of letting go of and removing from your life.

Keep in mind that there are certain things in our life that must be let go of until we are fully free of them, possibly even thousands of times. Forgive yourself during this process, moving on is one of the very hardest activities to engage with.

Stand up, with each of your feet just a little bit wider than the distance of your hips. Reach both of your arms over your head, interweave your fingers, and then extend each of your pointer fingers. When you inhale fresh air into your lungs, reach up high and exhale. Release all of your tension from your spirit. Do this ten times, then pause, the hand being help in a prayer position by your heart, feel the feeling of refreshment within you.

You have connected to your 3rd chakra now; your personal power has been enriched. Repeat this process multiple times to boost your confidence and ensure that you completely move on from whatever is holding you back.

You are able to change. You have the power.

Solar Plexus (2)

Get yourself into a comfortable position. If you are laying the floor, allow your entire body to fully relax and come into heightened awareness. Leave all of your negative worries and thoughts at the door; this moment is uniquely set out just for you and your personal power.

Acknowledge any sounds that exist inside an outside of the room. Rest in awareness of the room's temperature without judgment. Let all of these thoughts, feelings, and emotions go.

Now, bring all of your soft attention to your solar plexus region. Visualize a beautiful yellow light this light is your Manipura- your personal power and confidence.

How big is this light? Can you feel its energy? Or is it just soft energy? Now allow this light to pass over your entire body and provide warmth with comfort to you. (Repeat these questions in your mind without judgment).

Feel your body becoming more relaxed and embracing feelings of comfort and calm. Your spirit is being strengthened from within as you let go of the past and embrace the new power unleashed within you. Your 3rd chakra, the chakra of your self-belief and personal power is being infused with your spirit.

Bring your attention to your physical sensations now. Start to feel your feet on the floor and hands in your lap. When you are ready, open your eyes and rise.

Heart Chakra Meditation (Meditation time approx. 15 when repeated 2 times)

This chakra translates directly to "unhurt." This particular chakra is where one's love, kindness, and compassion to themselves and others are found and empowered. This chakra is fairly easy to understand because it is concerned with love in our hearts for others, us, and our circumstances. In this way, this chakra is associated with healing one's pain and instilling health.

Get yourself into a comfortable position. If you are laying on the floor, allow your entire body to relax and become comfortable fully. If you are sitting in a chair, settle your hands on your thighs or at the side of your body.

Now, close your eyes. This time if uniquely set out for you. Leave all of your worries. Let them go.

Have awareness for all of the sounds that surround you; just allow them to be present without judgment or interaction.

Be aware of the shade and light permeating through your eyelids. Feel the soft cool air softly touching your body's surface.

Sense the massive sky above you, along with the broad horizons that stretch around you, feel the earth below you, supporting your weight and body.

Draw in a breath that cleanses you and then breath out all of the tension that has built up inside of your body and mind. Let your breath fall naturally into a rhythm. When thoughts arise, acknowledge them and let them go. You are not a victim of your thoughts. You are a strong and non-judgmental observer. Breathe in and breathe out (repeat with rhythm).

Draw your attention to your chest region. Visualize a beautiful green light in this area, swirling in a circular fashion. How is this light functioning? Is it bright? Is it warm? Is there a tingle associated with this light? What are your thoughts at this moment?

Breathe in this green light all the way down into your hands and arms. Breathe this into your pelvis, toes and legs. Breath this light up into your chest, head, filling the body and connecting with every other chakra inside your spirit.

Now draw your focus to your chest area once again, to the circling green light chakra, notice a small pink rosebud in the very center. Le this pink rosebud unwind slowly, once petal at a time, and opening into a wonderful pink flower that is surrounded by a bright green light with a gold center.

Remind yourself that you are safe once you completely open your heart center to allow yourself to both receive and give others love. Once you breathe this light inward, it will accompany love and openness in your heart. When you breathe out, the green light will diminish all fear within you. Allow yourself to feel the beautiful green glow as it twirls and encompasses you.

Breathing this green light in, and breathing out tension. This is your focus. Repeat to yourself that you are loved and are indeed worthy of love. Breath in, breath out.

It is now time to close this chakra down. Bring all of your attention to your chest, right to the green light that is the Heart Chakra. See the twirling green light decreasing in size. Bring the size of this light down to a small light. Reduce this light to normal function. Repeat the mantra, "My Heart Chakra is operating normally."

Now, bring all of you awareness right back to the consistent flow of your breath. Breathe in and breathe out.

When you feel that you are ready, open your eyes.

Heart (2)

Find a comfortable seated position. Feel the soft connection of your body to the earth. Rooted to the earth in this way, let your spine drift upwards to the sky, extending to the top of your head. When you inhale, let your shoulders fall from your ears in a gentle manner, allow them to rest softly down your back. Feel the collarbones widen, and your heart opens up.

Now, start watching the subtle flow of life that is breathing through your entire body. You have now become an observer of every way that your body moves you become filled with the force of life.

Now we will start a breathing exercise that will cleanse your nervous system and pride balances all of your body's systems. Start by making a "Peace sign" with your fingers and the place each of the fingertips at the center of the third eye. Next, use your thumb to close your right nostril and then breath deep into your belly through only the left nostril. At the very top of the breath, pause and then close the left nostril and exhale through the right. Allow the inhale and exhale on both sides to be of the exact same length. Use the mantra "I am" when inhaling and "Love" when exhaling.

Now, allow yourself to think of a time when you had received love unconditionally from someone else or when you had given it to another person. Start fostering these feelings that you felt when you were given this love. Whatever emotions manifest, feel them and express gratitude for them.

Allow these feelings to flow into your heart. Now, visualize the center of your heart space and a bright glowing green light.

As this light spins brightly, feel the heart being cleansed of self-doubt, envy and pain toward yourself or others. Release and be cleansed of everything that is no longer serving you. Continue breathing in a harmonious rhythm. Invite these native emotions to be released and accept feelings of peace, joy and passion into each and every one of your cells.

Visualize the roots of these positive emotions flowing to the very root of your spine and into the center of the earth.

Gently begin blinking your eyes as you allow yourself to feel the physical sensations of your feet on the floor and hands in your lap.

Now, open your eyes and rise.

Throat Chakra Meditation (Meditation time approx. 15 when repeated 3 times)

This chakra translates to "very pure." Notably, the Throat chakra provides a voice to one's personalized truths. Where does one's voice stem from? Where does this energy emirate from? Physically, the answer is clearly the throat. However, as far as your energy is concerned, this energy stems from one's 5th chakra. Indeed, this chakra allows you to express your own truth in a clarified manner.

Get into a comfortable position. You can be seated or lying on the floor, while you let your whole body fall into a peaceful state of relaxation.

Now, close your eyes. Take in a cleansing breath and gently observe the natural rhythm of your breathing. Breathe in and breathe out. Allow thoughts to come and go without judgment. This is your time. Gently repeat the rhythm of your breathing in harmony and serenity.

Bring all of your attention to your throat. Visualize a beautiful small blue light; this light is twirling in a circle.

Observe and accept how this feels without judgment. With every, inhale of air visualize yourself breathing in more blue light. This blue light is filling your Throat Chakra and your neck region, spreading through your entire body and illuminating your spirit. This blue light spreads into your legs and hands. Feelings of relaxation are spreading through you now. This light is connecting with all of your other chakras.

As you inhale, this blue turquoise light provides truth and compassion for listening.
When you exhale, this turquoise blue light will remove everything that is blocking your spirt. All negative

emotions are cast out. This peaceful blue glow spins and encompasses every aspect of you. Remind yourself that your spirit is connected to truth and clarity. Inhale Blue light, exhale tension and inner chaos. Repeat this action.

Now, visualize this blue light, and see it opening in a similar way to a flower. This light stretches far from you but remains connected to your spirit. You will now see the energy and light of positivity and guidance from the Divine that is seeping into you abundantly. Keep this image in your mind for 10 seconds. Count in the rhythm of your breath.

It is not time to close this chakra. Bring all of your attention to your chest region. See the twirling blur light diminishing in size. Repeat to yourself, "My Throat Chakra is operating normally. Its function is normal."

Return all of your power for awareness to the flow of the breath. Breathing in and out in rhythm and harmony. Notice the natural flow of your stomach as you inhale and exhale with every breath.

Bring your attention to your body now. Feel the physical sensations of your body connected to the floor and your hands in your lap.

When you are fully ready, open your eyes and rise.

Throat (2)

Take a deep breath, extend this breath and then exhale. When you exhale, shift all of your attention to your throat. Visualize a blue light glowing as your chakra. This chakra now spreads in a vibrating harmony, like a pulse, from your throat to fully fill your neck and head. Now it moves to fill the rest of your body.

Imagine that you are strolling through a forest on a very small path. This pathway is lined on each side by massive trees that offer shade from the sun. Now, you can hear the sounds of small bugs and animals moving around. Birds are chirping as well. Far in this distance, a gentle stream flows over a rock bed and is making a soft flowing sound.

You now come across a narrow clearing that sits along with a huge log with a brush covered floor. You stroll next to it and sit down with your back gently against the log.

The forest's sounds are clearer in this position. These sounds carry a special meaning and you are able to hear them along with sounds that are fainter. This entire forest is playing music just for you.

Your fifth chakra is twirling and building its strength within you. It starts to spin faster; a gentle blue light starts to wash over your body and enters every cell and every single pore within the body.

Take a deep breath, and allow yourself to fully feel the energy that funnels through your throat, which is burning with a bright blue light.

Rest in this awareness. Now, stand up and begin walking from the log that has fallen at the very edge of the forest. This is where you first started. Take a gaze back at the forest that is signing just for you.

When you feel fully ready, open up your eyes and rise.

Third Eye Chakra Meditation (Meditation time approx. 15 when repeated 2 times)

This chakra translates to "beyond wisdom." The function of this chakra is to open your mind to information that is beyond simply the material world and your 5 senses. Enhanced sensory perception, intuition and or psychic energy are all derived from the 3rd eye. There is a small land in your eye that is shaped much like a pinecone that takes light in. This gland is called the pineal gland and is responsible for helping you feel awake in during the day and tired at nightfall. Ancient cultures, far before modern brain imaging, were privy to the existence of the third eye, realizing that it receives information from sources that are outside of our 5 senses.

Find a place where you are completely comfortable and will not be disturbed. Wear loose or unrestrictive clothing and turn down the lighting if it is too bright.

Start with a deep inhale and breathe through your nose. Hold this for a short period and then release it gently through the mouth. When you do this, feel a sense of relaxation to come over you.

Let go of thoughts that enter your mind that heighten fear and doubt about yourself and others. Inhale through the nose and exhale through the mouth. When you exhale, let go of fears that exist within your mind.

This process is natural and very safe. The gold light will place you in a more polished frequency where there are only positive experiences. Now, relax and let these experiences happen.

Let the golden circle of light within your forehead to completely open and send gentle rays of light in every direction. Let this light relax you fully.

Allow your body to fall into more relaxation. Further into relaxation with every breath.

Feel that your body is becoming light, your weight is decreasing, and you will fall into a state of relaxation. More light will begin to flow right into your third eye and all throughout your entire body.

Completely let go of all uncertainty. All questions of doubt are released into the atmosphere and fully released from you with every breath.

Allow yourself to open your third eye in a natural way... now you will relax in a complete way... feeling more and more relaxed as the golden light of the third eye flows out from your forehead.

Third eye (2)

For this meditation, there will be 24 steps split into 3 days for added benefit and to aid your grasp of the benefits that it has to offer.

Find a place where you are completely comfortable and will not be disturbed. Wear loose or unrestrictive clothing and turn down the lighting if it is too bright.

This third eye meditation will progress slowly and provide ample time for you to settle in and enjoy the experience.

Start with a deep inhale and breathe through your nose. Hold this for a short period and then release it gently through the mouth. When you do this, feel a sense of relaxation to come over you.

Allow your face to fully relax, unclenching your jaw and letting all of the muscles in your face to relax.

With this, your body will soon to begin to relax as well. You may feel a sense of warmth coming over you.

Welcome this relaxation to spread over your entire body and increasing as it moves more deeply through you.

Bring all of your attention right between your eyebrows. Rest in awareness of your Third Eye. This is the energy within the forehead, this radiates and opens light. Visualize a gentle image of light nearly the size of a golf ball that radiates gold light similar to the sun. This light will radiate in all directions around you.

Steady your breath and visually this light surrounding you from your Center. Repeat this over and over until you feel the warmth completely encompass you. Repeat this process 10 times. Feel this energy around you.

When you are ready, open your eyes and rise.

Crown Chakra Meditation (Meditation time approx. 10 when repeated 3 times)

This chakra can be translated to, "thousand petaled." As such, this chakra is the energy of pure consciousness. Moreover, this chakra is a noticeable difficult energy to fully explain in a manner that is not convoluted or interwoven with pedantic syntax. Think of this energy as analogous to magnetism. The color of this chakra is violet-white, and its Center is found at the very top of the head. The energy of this chakra radiates between one's eyes, extending in an infinite manner outward and upward, and then connecting you to the rest of the universe's energy.

If you can, hike all the way to the summit of a particular place, this can be a mountain, a roof, etc.) Bring a blanket, flowers, and possible matches and a candle as well. The goal here is to create a sacred space for yourself.

Peacefully place your blanket on the ground, and put the altar together as you contemplate the meaning that all of these items have to you.

Take up a cross-legged seat on top of your blanket. Now, put your left hand over the heart area on your chest. Gently place your right fingertips on the ground beside you.

Close your eyes and fall into a natural comfort into your seated position. Feel your deep connection to the earth. Let you back, and spine rise with the top of your head rise to the sky.

Now, connect to the natural flow of your breath. Allow yourself to feel the special value of this connection immediately.

Feel each falling and rising of your body with each breath. Every breath comes and goes, experience this fully. Rest in the awareness of the belief that there is a life force that is breathing in and out of you. Something deeper than you that resides within you.

This very force is giving you all of the breath that is needed to maintain your life. This force is within and around your entire existence. This force is everything, everything beyond your body and your life.

Open yourself to the possibility of being connected to this force. You can name this spirit anything you wish: God, Life, Mother...

Recognize the presence at this moment. Embrace its energy.

When you are ready, take one last deep breath. Open your eyes and rise into the rest of your day.

Body Scan (10 mins. Repeat 5x)

Feel your feet rested comfortably on the floor.

Feel the cold air inhaled through your nostrils

Notice any unique bodily sensations that you are feeling

When you are distracted or lost in thought, bring your attention right back to your breath

Feel the rise and fall of your chest as you inhale and exhale

Feel and notice where the movement of your breath is felt in your body

Notice the influx of thoughts and then return to a bodily sensation or the breath

Notice where your body is uneasy or uncomfortable

Notice whether your breaths are shallow or deep without changing them

Move continually from the top of your head down to the soles of your feet

Allow the pain and discomfort to pass through your body and let it go.

Finally, if you found this book useful in any way, a review on Amazon is always appreciated!

Guided Self-Healing and Mindfulness Meditations Bundle:

Multiple Meditation Scripts such as Chakra Healing, Breathing Meditation, Body Scan Meditation, Vipassana, and Self-Hypnosis for a Better Life!

By Healing Meditation Academy

Table of Contents

Guided Meditations for Mindfulness and Self Healing
Chapter 1: Mindfulness Meditation

Beginner Breathing (10 minutes if done individually)

The Stimulating Breath: The aim here is to enhance your overall alertness and internal energy sources.

The 4-7-8 Exercise

Breathing Exercise Three:

Breathe Counting
Anger Relaxation
Grief Relaxation

Chapter 2: Chakra Healing Meditation

Root Chakra Meditation (Meditation time approx. 15 when repeated 2 times)

Root (2)

Sacral Chakra Meditation (Meditation time approx. 15 when repeated 2 times)

Sacral Chakra (2)

Solar Plexus Meditation (Meditation time approx. 15 when repeated 3 times)

Solar Plexus (2)

Heart Chakra Meditation (Meditation time approx. 15 when repeated 2 times)

Heart (2)

Throat Chakra Meditation (Meditation time approx. 15 when repeated 3 times)

Throat (2)

Third Eye Chakra Meditation (Meditation time approx. 15 when repeated 2 times)

Third eye (2)

Crown Chakra Meditation (Meditation time approx. 10 when repeated 3 times)

Body Scan (10 mins. Repeat 5x)

Guided Self-Healing and Mindfulness Meditations Bundle:

Table of Contents

Breathing Meditation

Easy Breathing Meditation to Improve Mindfulness
Diaphragm Meditation for Panic Disorders
Relaxing the Body
Targeted Muscle Group Relaxation Script
Relaxation and Physical Hypnosis Meditation

Opening Awareness

Breathing Awareness and Control Meditation
Stress and Workplace Awareness Meditation

Abdominal Breathing

Abdominal Breathing for Oxygenation
Abdominal Breathing for Impulse Control

Loving and Kindness Meditation

Kindness Meditation for Self-Care
Love Meditation for Actualization

Self-Compassion "Break" Meditation

Forgiveness Guided Self-Healing

Universal Compassion Meditation

Vipassana Meditation

Anxiety Meditation

General Self-Healing Script for On-The-Spot Anxiety Relief
Guided Anxiety Meditation for Active Brains

Introduction

Think about the last time you left work, came home, and actually felt relaxed — not a half-relaxation filled with anxiety and thoughts about the next day – an actual, peaceful calm. For most of us, we might remember this sense of peace last in grade school, or perhaps further back. The pace of our modern world is incredibly fast, and most of us barely had time to notice that suddenly, all of our free time was occupied. Even when we aren't at work nine to five or studying at school – our brains are always working. Thinking. Constant stimuli can be great when it comes to keeping up with your loved ones, but the negative effects of the internet and social media particularly affect our day-to-day mindfulness. You can think of the definition of mindfulness as simply paying attention. Mindfulness places particular importance on focusing the mind, honing your concentration, and really emotionally connecting with what you're centered upon. Mindfulness can center upon anything you choose – if you're stressed about work, thinking clearly and directly about one specific problem can help you overcome it. Meditation comes into play with mindfulness at this stage of thinking clearly and directly. Most of us have, at any given time, more than a handful of things on our minds. Meditating allows you to use your concentration for whittling that handful down. Once you learn how to meditate to quiet your thoughts in order to focus directly on a mindful pursuit, you won't believe the changes you'll experience. Meditation for mindfulness has proven to help individuals be more productive, live their lives with a more positive outlook, and think in healthier thought patterns. Whether you experience anxiety, stress, depression, or simply fatigue from your day-to-day life, taking a moment to compose your thoughts and sink into a deep concentration will abate your symptoms. Many doctors and psychiatrists prescribe meditation with a mindfulness focus as a means of controlling or dealing with difficult life stressors. In order to determine the type of meditation that's right for you, this helpful guide will walk through all the most popular, and effective, style of meditation. Complete with full scripts that will help you center yourself, calm your negative emotions, and bring you peace, each of the following chapters contains everything you need to know about self-healing with guided mindfulness meditations. If you're ready to get started breathing, centering, and freeing your mind, let's dive into the meditation methods that are going to change your life.

Breathing Meditation

Easy Breathing Meditation to Improve Mindfulness

Come into your breath, and your breath will ground you.

Learning to ground your spirit keeps your being whole.

Approach your meditation with an open chest –

Here is air, and there is life.

Allow yourself to settle into a comfortable position, palms open, body relaxed, and stable.

You are in control – it is time to discover the power of your breath.

As you sit, quiet, still, listen to your heart.

Hear the drum – slow, steady. You are a cycle, a pattern, a song.

Inhale for four counts – one, two, three, four,

And exhale for four counts – one, two, three, four.

Your breath brings your life.

Focus all of your mindful attention on the give and take of breathing.

Inhale for one, two, three, four,

And exhale for one, two, three, and four.

Inhale for one, two, three, four,

And exhale for one, two, three, and four.

As you inhale, imagine the universe swelling inside you –

All consuming, you breathe in – and become one.

Inhale for one, two, three, and four –

And exhale for one, two, three, and four – breathe out thanks.

Breathe out appreciation.

Your body, mind, and spirit come alive only with your breath –

And the universe is here to provide for you.

Inhale for one, two, three, four,

And exhale, complete, for one, two, three, four.

Once more, listen to the beating of your heart –

Take three more breaths, focusing on a silent mind and peaceful body.

Inhale for one, two, three, four,

And exhale, for one, two, three, four.

Inhale for one, two, three, four,

And exhale, for one, two, three, four.

Inhale for one, two, three, and four.

True breath brings true peace.

You have centered your breath. Inhale, and exhale, one final time.

Slowly open your eyes. Allow your breath to remain steady.

Go forward.

Diaphragm Meditation for Panic Disorders

You are in control.

There is nothing that can take away your power.

Focus your mind upon only your chest.

Inhale for one, two, three, four,

And exhale for one, two, three, and four.

You are in control.
You are in control.

Call out to your mindful brain –

It is always there, even when you feel overwhelmed.

Call out – focus on finding your mindfulness.

Allow your spirit to quiet.

Inhale for one, two, three, four,

And exhale, for one, two, three, four.

Panic has no place here.

Fear has no place here.

Feel only your breath.

Let your inhales and exhales slow your heart rate.

Breathe in for one, two, three, four,

And expel your anxiety in exhalation – one, two, three, four.

Breathe in for one, two, three, four,

And expel your fear in exhalation – one, two, three, four.

Breathe in for one, two, three, four,

And expel your insecurity in exhalation – one, two, three, four.

Each breath brings life into your being,

Each exhalation takes the pain from your spirit.

Feel your heart rate slowing.

You are calm and in control.

Inhale for one, two, three, four,

And exhale for one, two, three, and four.

As you begin to calm, focus on your lower stomach.

Feel the motion of your diaphragm as you inhale –

One, two, three, four,

And exhale – one, two, three, and four.

Your breath, heart, and belly are your spirit, mind, and body.

Feel your unified being come to peace.

There is no need for fear.
There is no need for anxiety.
Feel your breath.
Inhale – one, two, three, four,
Exhale – one, two, three, four.
Inhale – one, two, three, four,
Exhale – one, two, three, four.
Give yourself permission to find peace.
You do not need to worry.
You do not need to panic.
All is right when your being is centered.
Feel your mindful brain relax,
Inhale for one, two, three, four,
And exhale for one, two, three, and four.
You are light and peaceful – you are safe.
Breathe in for three deep breaths,
And cultivate a safe space for your most anxious moments.
Inhale for one, two, three, four,
And exhale for one, two, three, and four.
With each breath, you solidify the safety of your space.

You are here and protected – in your own existence.
Inhale for one, two, three, four,
And exhale, for one, two, three, four.
Inhale for one, two, three, four,
And exhale, for one, two, three, four.
As you calm and gently move towards surfacing consciousness,
Remember this space you have created.
Hold your peaceful safety sacred –
This cultivated sanctuary is yours.
Any time you feel overwhelmed, return to it.
Return to your mind.
Return to your breath.
Return to your center.
Open your eyes, and go forth with strength
And peace.

Relaxing the Body

When it comes to practicing bodily guided self-healing meditations, the basic outline you'll want to follow is one of focusing, tensing, and relaxing. When you do a bodily relaxation meditation for self-healing, you'll be taking stock of every muscle, system, and reaction. Our bodies can sometimes suffer daily damage that we aren't even aware of. Most individuals hold tension in their jaws, teeth, hands, and shoulders. When you do a bodily relaxation meditation, you will silently take stock of each of your body's aches and pains – in an attempt to relax and bring yourself peace where you need it most. Let's start with a very simple, slow meditation that you can do when you get into bed each night before you go to sleep. Bodily meditations have the added bonus of relaxing your physical being, as well as your emotional side so that you are much more likely to drift into a deep sleep. Once you're ready for bed, lay down on your back with your arms by your side, palms facing downwards on your mattress, legs slightly parted. You can feel free to adjust your position to what's most comfortable for you. However, you should focus on being prone and in a position you routinely like to rest in. On your back is the best possible way to lay with an open chest, an open heart, and an aligned physical being before you begin your meditation – but not everyone's physical body is the same. Find your comfort, and we'll begin. With your eyes closed, walk yourself through the following meditation either once or twice, depending on your body's overall stress and tension.

Targeted Muscle Group Relaxation Script

As your day comes to a close, open your heart and mind to full relaxation.

Gently close your eyes. Feel the dark settle around you like a blanket.

Breathe in through your nose, for one, two, three, four –

And breathe out through your mouth, for one, two, three, four.

Let each exhalation countdown expel negative energy with your breath.

Feel the blood running through your body as you breathe in,

One, two, three, four;

And let your stress and tension dissipate as you breathe out –

One, two, three, four.

You are here, present, and ready for rest.

Let your brain quiet. Focus only on your breath.

Feel your muscles relax as your body fills with oxygen.

Think down to your toes.

What did you do on your feet today?

Are they sore or tired? Focus on your feet.

As you exhale, prepare to tighten your toes as you breathe in.

Inhale one, two, three, four, and squeeze your toes at tight as you can.

Slowly release, exhale one, two, three, four.

Feel the tension in your toes come undone.

Breathe in, one, two, three, four, and shift your focus to your calves.

Exhale one, two, three, four, and tighten your calves as you begin to inhale.

One, two, three, four, tighter, tighter –

And release, for one, two, three, four.

As you move upwards through your muscles, concentrate only on the weight of your own body.

Here, you are present with your spirit, mind, and being.

Each clench and release helps free you from stress.

It is safe to let go. You are allowed to relax.

Think about your knees. Are they tight, or sore?

As you inhale, tighten your knees for one, two, three, and four –

And slowly release, for one, two, three, four.

As you release your knees, press your palms down and feel the ground.

You are here, and your knees, although meant for walking,

Are here to rest.

Think about your thighs. Breathe in and tense, one, two, three, and four –

And slowly release, one, two, three, and four.

Half the tension in your body has dissolved.

You are halfway to a peaceful sleep.

Refocus your mind if your thoughts wander, and think about your glutes.

Did you sit today? Are you tense?

Breathe in and squeeze for one, two, three, and four –

And release for one, two, three, and four.

Your abdomen is the heart of your center.

Slow your muscles slow your breath and pause.

Listen to the sound of your heartbeat.

Your body keeps your heart and spirit safe.

Rejuvenation is key.

Think about your lower back.

Tight, tense, sore.

Breathe in and tighten for one, two, three, four,

And release for one, two, three, and four.

Shift your focus from back to front.

Think about your abdominal muscles.

Think about your stomach.

On an inhale, tighten one, two, three, four,

 Squeezing your abs at the top of the inhale.

Release slowly and exhale out, one, two, three, and four.

You are almost done. Feel your muscles nearing sleep.

Moving upwards, focus on your shoulders.

Let them relax, allow them to heal.

Tense and hold for one, two, three, four,

And exhale your release, one, two, three, and four.

Focus once more on the tightness in your shoulders.

This time, press them back into your mattress –

Open your heart and center to full surrender.

Breathe in for one, two, three, and four –

And out for one, two, three, and four.

Come slowly back to rest in a gentle prone position.

Follow your bloodstream down, down –

Towards the tips of your fingers at the tips of your arms.

They are tense like your toes and ready to rest.

Clench your fists as you inhale for one, two, three,

And slowly release your grasp, exhaling one, two, three, and four.

Up from your fingers, focus on your forearms.

Breathe in and squeeze your forearms for one, two, three, four,

And release for one, two, three, and four.

Next, move towards your biceps, up, up.

Flex and clench for one, two, three, and four -

And release – for one, two, three, four.

As we move toward your neck, feel the rest of your body lighten like air.

You are weightless. You are floating.

There is no physical attachment.

You are relaxed, and you are whole.

Breathe in and tense your shoulders up around your neck –

One, two, three, four.

And down, for one, two, three, four.

Shift your focus to your facial muscles. Here, tension is thick.

Through your jaw and mouth, we tend to hold stress.

Feel the muscles in your face, feel your breath entering and exiting your body.

Exist here for a moment, without any motion but breath.

Inhale, one, two, three, four – and exhale one, two, three, four.

Bring yourself down to your center.

Feel your spirit settle.

On your inhale, tighten your facial muscles for one, two, three, and four –

And release for one, two, three, and four.

Once more, return to your bloodstream. You are tired –

Your muscles have calmed,

Your soreness is gone,

There is no more tension.

You are light as air.

As you inhale, think of your body as one complete space.

A unit. A machine.

Your temple.

Exhale one, two, three, and four – and relax.

Sleep comes heavy.

Inhale one, two, three, four, and think about your entire being.

Exhale for one, two, three, and four and feel your breath leave your body.

Your toes, your abdomen, your neck, arms, and legs –

All are at peace.

Inhale, one, two, three, four – and tighten your entire body.

Hold for one, two, three, and exhale –

One, two, three, four.

Let your spirit sleep.

Let your mind rest.

Your physical body is purified.

Think of your palms as you drift off to sleep, pressed against your grounding force.

You are centered. All is quiet.

Allow yourself to sleep.

Relaxation and Physical Hypnosis Meditation

Give yourself permission to engage in self-care.

Find a position in which you are relaxed, comfortable, and open to the universe.

Wherever you find yourself, keep your palms open –

You are receptive to positive energy.

Relaxation of the body and mind rejuvenates the soul.

You are deserving of quiet, and you are deserving of peace.

Now is the time to relax.

Allow your eyelids to droop as you relax your jaw.

Seek out your breath, in through your nose, and out through your mouth.

Hear only the rush of your lifeline breath –

Inhale for one, two, three, and four;
And exhale for one, two, three, and four.
Let the pattern of your breath slow your heart rate.
Feel your toes, legs, and arms fill with air –
Oxygen will help you heal.
Open your heart to a mindful center;
Relaxation only comes once the tension has left.
Imagine, in your mind,
You are a vessel filled with water.
When you begin each day,
You are clear and clean – soft, smooth, still.
The surface is broken, your depths are pure.
There is nothing but love and calm.
As the day goes on,
Your peaceful vessel begins to bubble,
Slowly at first –
A bubble of anger, a rush of anxiety,
A pop of stress.

Your vessel stirs; you are no longer peaceful.

Throughout your day, more and more impurities

Bubble inside you.

Pressure, building, building, building.

Focus your mind on the top of your head.

At the end of the day, you are tight and ready to burst.

There is nothing peaceful about this pressure.

Inhale for four counts – one, two, three, four,

And exhale for four counts – one, two, three, four.

As you exhale, release your vessel's lid –

Allow the pressure to escape.

From your chin to your scalp, release your impurities like carbonated bubbles –

Inhale for one, two, three, four,

And exhale your pressure – one, two, three, four.

Focus on your abdomen, filled with bubbles – tight with pressure.

Release it, up, up, through your scalp, through your mind, out of your being forever.

Inhale for one, two, three, four,

And exhale tension – one, two, three, four.

You are a teapot giving off steam.

From the tips of your fingers up through your arms,

Release the pressure –

Inhale for one, two, three, four,

And exhale for one, two, three, and four.

From the lengths of your legs and up through your torso,

Release the pressure –

Inhale for one, two, three, four,

And exhale, for one, two, three, four.

From the tips of your toes to the top of your head –

Release the pressure.

Purify yourself.

Inhale for one, two, three, four,
And exhale for one, two, three, and four.
Allow your mindful brain to rest; your body is at peace.
All the difficult emotions bubbled up inside you have gone.
You are calm, serene.
You are filled with beautiful water – cool, peaceful, and clean.
There is nothing negative to weigh you down anymore,
You are light and airy,
Soft and clean.
Allow yourself to feel restful.
Allow yourself to feel at home.
Slowly, bring yourself back to consciousness.
You have purified and cleansed.
You are whole again.

Opening Awareness

Plenty of us are too bogged down in our personal lives, work lives, and social lives to realize that we have closed off our senses to awareness. Awareness in mindfulness and meditation often coincides with individuals who wish to control depression or anxiety. While awareness meditations aren't a total cure for these types of emotional disorders, opening your heart and mind to being aware of yourself, your surroundings, and your day to day life can have a huge impact on your happiness. Oftentimes referred to as a "frame shift," awareness will bond

Breathing Awareness and Control Meditation

Come to a comfortable position that allows your body to relax and rest.

Let your cheeks droop. Feel the tension in your jaw begin to dissipate.

Allow your eyelids to close, or if you're comfortable, keep them open.

Your meditation is your personal space.

As you open your heart to self-awareness today,

Picture yourself at the top of a mountain.

Here you are far away from your center –

High above the ground, anxious, and unaware.

But the comfort of solid ground is within your grasp.

With each number from ten to one, imagine yourself taking a step.

Closer, forwards, towards something better.

Ten.

Take a step. Feel your body accepting rest.

Nine.

Take a step. Feel your mind begin to slow.

Eight.

Take a step. With every number, you sink closer into deep awareness.

Seven.

Take a step and listen to your breath – your shallow gasps have changed to long, deep inhales. You're approaching your center.

Six.

The top of your journey is far behind you, and the tension you held has left.

Inhale for four counts – one, two, three, and four –

And exhale for four counts – one, two, three, four.

Take your last five steps, and with each one, give yourself over to complete surrendered awareness.

Five…four…three…two…one.

Here is your spiritual center. You are grounded, mentally, but you have not grounded your physical being.

Let us return to your awareness and return to your breath.

There is no fear of awareness – only acceptance and knowledge.

Feel the shallow inhale of your breath.

You have not found your breathing center.

Awareness will help you find it, and in turn, will bring you healing.

Take a deep breath in through your nose for one, two, three, four,

Extending your stomach outwards like a reach.

Breathe out now, through your mouth, one, two, three, four,

Collapsing your stomach against your spine.

You are a breathing being – breath is your life.

Focus your awareness. Focus your breathing. You are in control.

Calm any external thoughts – exhale them with your breath.

You are in the presence of your own spirit, and your breath brings it life.

Inhale for one, two, three, and four –

And exhale, for one, two, three, four.
As you inhale, search for knowledge.
One, two, three, four –
Survey your body while you exhale for one, two, three, and four.

If there is tension, seek it out.
Where there is a pain, find it.
Inhale for one, two, three, and four –
And exhale for one, two, three, and four.
Focus your awareness upon that which isn't aligned with your center.

Inhale and feel the tension – one, two, three, four.

Exhale, and purge your system of impurities.

Keep your mind and thoughts centered upon your misalignment –

For three deep breaths, allow your mindful state to focus only here.

Breathe and purge.

Inhale your tension – one, two, three, and four –

And exhale unnecessary stress for one, two, three, and four.

Inhale for one, two, three, and four;
And exhale for one, two, three, and four.
Inhale for one, two, three, and four;
And exhale for one, two, three, and four.
Your awareness no longer belongs to this region –

You have focused, found, and freed.

Return, now, to your ten-step journey.

You begin your ascent cleansed and clean.

Step forwards, up. One.

Feel your strength. Reaching the peak is no longer difficult.

Two. Higher, stronger. You are aware. You are calm.

Three. Four. Take a breath.

Inhale for one, two, three, four,
And exhale for one, two, three, and four.
Step up. Five. Six. Seven.
Up, eight. Nine. Ten.
Inhale for one, two, three, four,
And exhale for one, two, three, and four.

You have returned, but you are not the same.

You are centered. You have control.

Open your eyes slowly – awareness is a gift.

Stress and Workplace Awareness Meditation

As you enter into your meditative practice today, settle in a comfortable position that won't require shifting.

With your palms open and relaxed wherever you feel most natural,

Allow your eyelids to droop if they feel heavy, or gently flutter open if you prefer.

Through your nose, inhale for four counts – one, two, three, four,

And exhale for four counts out your mouth – one, two, three, four.

Self-healing doesn't always involve the self; as you calm your thoughts,

Focus your mindfulness on stress – work, school, errands, and deadlines.

Focus your mindfulness on stress – work, school, errands, and deadlines.

Inhale for one, two, three, four,

And exhale for one, two, three, and four.

Your stress is an elevator on the top floor –

Suspended, heavy, damage-inflicting.

You begin high up, caught, and trapped.

Inhale for one, two, three, four,

And exhale for one, two, three, and four.

As your mindfulness stretches to wrap around your stress,

Feel the burden deep inside you.

To rid yourself of negativity, you must first root out its cause.

Where do you feel that your stress comes from?

Are you too busy at work? Anxious? Tired? Find your cause.

Find your root.

Inhale for one, two, three, four,

And exhale for one, two, three, and four.

Fixate on the cause of your imbalance – stress cannot come from where it doesn't belong.

Negative emotions have no place in your mental space.

Leave work at work – allow yourself the luxury of a safe place.

Inhale for one, two, three, four,

And exhale for one, two, three, and four.

Move your elevator down one floor. Heavy, difficult – but relief is close.

Feel your burden lighten – feel your spirits rise as tension falls.

You are closer to the floor, no longer dangerously on edge.

The cable above your head no longer strains with stress – but your mind remains tight.

Move gently down another floor, your mechanism creaking, shaking, but relaxing.

Your elevator cannot fall if you have brought it to the ground.

Inhale for one, two, three, four,
And exhale for one, two, three, and four.
Stress can spill over to become anxiety or anger – bring your elevator down, and allow this floor to purge your negative emotions.
Here, you are angry, hurt, embarrassed – overworked, tired, disillusioned.
You cannot stay. And you won't.
Leave behind these dangerous emotions – if they build too strongly, your elevator crashes.
Self-healing takes times, and self-healing takes strength.
Do not let your stress prove you weak.
Pull your elevator down again, inhaling for one, two, three four,
Exhaling negativity for one, two, three, and four.
Feel your breath, like your elevator, push the pain aside.
You cannot control what causes you stress, but you can help your mind bring your spirit back to the center.

There is no time for undue stress that we cannot ourselves change.

Pull down again, another floor. Each is softer, each is easier.

Your elevator plays your music – allow yourself to relax.

Inhale for one, two, three, four,

And exhale for one, two, three, and four.

With one final pull, bring your elevator down to the ground floor.

Inhale your safe solid state - one, two, three, four;

And exhale your doubt - one, two, three, four.

Steady your mind, and clear away any thoughts of work or stress.

You are centered here. Give no more of your time to stress.

Your minutes are yours, your thoughts are yours, and your elevator is yours.

Inhale for one, two, three, four,

And exhale for one, two, three, and four.

Here, your journey ends and begins. You are centered and grounded, spiritually and physically. Only you can allow your elevator to be drug back up.

Hold your ground – you are in control.

Inhale for one, two, three, four,

And exhale for one, two, three, and four.

Go mindfully into your stressful spaces with the center, control, and focus.

Slowly, open your eyes, and allow yourself to exist stress-free.

Abdominal Breathing

Abdominal breathing, unlike breathing meditation, focuses a bit more on your physical muscles than on your spiritual and emotional breathing as it relates to your inner peace. Abdominal breathing meditations are helpful in allowing your body to fill your bloodstream with oxygen – which creates, in turn, an incredible sense of calm, fulfillment, and bodily health. Most of us have no idea how to breathe properly using our diaphragm muscles, nose, and mouth – we simply do our best, without learning the proper technique to maximize our airflow and really enrich your body with oxygenated biological mindfulness. In order to properly meditate with abdominal breathing techniques, you're going to want to focus on breathing in through your nose, and out through your mouth. It might not sound very complicated, but the basic idea behind abdominal breathing meditations is to hone your breath to treat your body better. When you breathe in through your nose, to properly engage your diaphragm, you have to extend your stomach out and downwards, as if you are pressing the oxygen down into the lowest part of your belly. Once you've completed your inhale, you should collapse your stomach in an upwards motion while exhaling through your mouth. Instead of filling your belly to the very bottom, your exhale should be about starting from the bottom and pushing the oxygen out. Try this pattern a few times, and once you get the hang of it, you should start to feel your body tingle, relax, and fill with oxygen. When your bloodstream is highly oxygenated, your brain, heart, muscles, and organs function more effectively. Let's walk through a quick abdominal breathing meditation to teach you how to move your diaphragm, before getting into a full abdominal breathing mindfulness meditation script.

When you engage in abdominal breathing meditation, you'll want to make sure you are positioned so that your spine is straight and your upper abdomen isn't bent in a way that obstructs your airways. While most individuals choose to sit down in a comfortable cross-legged position on a soft matt or pillow, everyone is different – as long as your airways aren't being constricted, your abdominal breathing will function normally. Close your eyes, and let us begin.

Abdominal Breathing for Oxygenation

Relax. Feel your body enter into a mindful state.

Allow your heart to begin self-healing.

Your only focus now is breath.

In, and out.

In, and out.

Feel your heartbeat.

Inhale slowly through your nose,

Extending your stomach outwards for one, two, three.

Exhale slowly through your mouth, as you push

Your breath for three, two, one, up and out.

You collapse only to open – feel the cycle.

Inhale again, this time pushing your air

Down low into your belly.
Exhale slowly, pushing from that same deep
Up from the bottom –
Three, two, one.
Feel your diaphragm stretch, contract, and shift.
You are breathing as the universe intended.
Allow your bloodstream to fill with oxygen –
Your breath is your life.
Inhale through your nose, one, two, three, four,
Pushing your stomach out-outs,
Then exhale slowly, through your mouth,
One, two, three, four,
Pushing up – up, breathing with your diaphragm.
Center your focus on breathing only,
Your stomach, out, diaphragm, up,
Over and over, a nourishing pattern.
Inhale for one, two, three, four,

And exhale for one, two, three, and four.
Inhale for one, two, three, four,
And exhale for one, two, three, and four.
Inhale for one, two, three, four,
And exhale for one, two, three, and four.

Feel your muscles begin to remember how to use your diaphragm.

With every breath, in and out, your body remembers how to breathe.

Deep, long, slow – strong.

Breathe with your whole body.

Inhale for one, two, three, four,

And out for one, two, three, and four.

Learning and teaching take patience –

You are both student and teacher.

Your body is strong,

You are filled with oxygen – your breath is your life.

Allow your muscles to work freely;

A freely breathing body brings levity to the soul.

Inhale for one, two, three, four,

And exhale for one, two, three, and four.

Remember the way your muscles work –
Remember the way your breath feels.
Inhale for one, two, three, four,
And exhale for one, two, three, and four.
Work your stomach, feel your abdominals.
You are mindful and aware – your breath has never been stronger.
Inhale for one, two, three, four,
And exhale for one, two, three, and four.
Let your mind control your body –
Let your body heal your spirit.
Inhale for one, two, three, four, remembering your movements.
Exhale for one, two, three, and four – a repeating pattern.
Your breath is ancient, a combination of all your body, mind, and spirit –
But you are mindful, and a mindful heart can train their breath.
Inhale for one, two, three, four,
And exhale for one, two, three, four – you are growing as you breathe.
Slowly allow your pace to loosen.

Release control over your breath.

Feel how your muscles recreate the pattern.

You now know your ancient breath – remind your body how to use it.

Abdominal Breathing for Impulse Control

Inhale naturally for four counts – one, two, three, four,

And exhale naturally for four counts – one, two, three, four.

Center your mindfulness on only your breath:

Are your inhales shallowly? Are your exhales short?

Center your mindfulness on only your spirit –

Allow your breath to draw out your negativity.

Bring to mind your stressors, but don't allow them to affect your center.

Hold your pain in focus – and breathe, slowly.
Inhale for one, two, three, four,
But exhale sharp, quick, fast –

Loving and Kindness Meditation

Kindness Meditation for Self-Care

Practicing kindness towards oneself take time and patience.

Approach your meditation today with an open heart – not for the world, but for yourself.

As you come to rest in a comfortable prone position, allow your eyes to gently close against your cheeks.

Feel the breath enter and exit your body – inhale for one, two, three, four,

And exhale, for one, two, three, four.

You are three beings together – spirit, body, and mind, and you must nurture each with kindness.

As you feel yourself settle into a mindful state, imagine you are sinking through the floor.

You are not heavy with burden, or heavy with pain –

Your spirit, body, and mind, are heavy with calm, and in practicing self-kindness, you invite peace to join you.

Inhale for one, two, three, four, and exhale, for one, two, three, four.

The rise of your chest brings life to all you are – but all you are sometimes can suffer from the stress of life.

You are gentle – and must treat yourself so.

Take your spirit, body, and mind into your hands, and allow your meditation to reinvigorate your being with kindness.

Shift your focus onto your center. Imagine, in the middle of your chest, a glowing light.

This light is your love for your own self – created within, and nurtured within.

Inhale for one, two, three, four, and watch your light grow.

Exhale for one, two, three, and four.

Inside your chest, your light is larger – brighter – kinder.

While you focus on enlarging the light inside your chest, breath in for one, two, three, four, and out, for one, two, three, and four.

Keep your palms open to the universe as you feed your inner light.

Inhale for one, two, three, four, glowing from arm to arm.

Exhale for one, two, three, four, and feel the light reach down to your fingers.

You are a being lit in kindness, kindness created by you, for you.

Once more breathe in for one, two, three, four, igniting your body in the light as you exhale – one, two, three, and four.

Wreath yourself in kindness. You are your best lover.

Turn your mindful brain inwards towards your spirit.

Send light in waves to bathe your passions, dedication, motivation, and satisfaction.

You deserve to be kind to yourself.

Move from your spirit onto your body.

Allow your light to warm.

Inhale for one, two, three, four, and feel the sun against your skin.

Exhale one, two, three, and four – and let your fingers tingle.

All across your physical being, send waves of light and kind intentions.

Our physical beings are often overlooked, but you cannot be whole without all three selves.

Your physical being keeps you alive. Your physical being keeps you safe.

Treat your body with love. Treat your body with kindness.

Cruel words cannot change what you cannot change – kindness is acceptance, and acceptance is self-love.

Breathe in for one, two, three, four,

And out for one, two, three, and four.

Turn now to your mind, that dusty place with anxious thoughts and sharp fears.

Your mind is sacred, the home of your creativity, yourself, and your drive.

Bathe your mind in kindness – you are smart, you are strong, and you are capable of anything.

Inhale for one, two, three, four,

And exhale for one, two, three, and four.

Once more take stock of the weight of your body – you are heavy, thick, laden down with density;

But it is all love.

You are heavy with love.

Kindness is not easily found outside, but instead better cultivated inside your mind.

You can glow, on your own, and heal, on your own.

You are spirited, body, and mind – and if you are kind, you can do anything.

Inhale for one, two, three, four, and feel your glow begin to lighten.

You are a beacon of kindness – and your work, for now, is finished.

Inhale for one, two, three, four,

And exhale one, two, three, and four.

Absorb the light you left behind, taking in what wasn't used.

Slowly, dimly, bring yourself to a soft low burn.

Your kindness is a lamp inside your chest.

Find its glow when you need it most, but never let the light die out.

Inhale for one, two, three, four,

And exhale, kind, lit in light, for one, two, three, and four.

Gently allow your eyes to open. You re-enter the world as one –

Kindness forged, you are spirit, body, and mind at peace.

Love Meditation for Actualization

Settle into yourself.

Allow your physical being to disconnect from your spirit.

Here, and now, you are two separations – a vessel and a traveler.

Sink down into a comfortable position.

Allow your eyes to shut gently, or lightly rest open on a gentle face.

Inhale for four counts – one, two, three, four,

And exhale for four counts – one, two, three, four.

Your rhythm is your guide. Let your breath relax your body.

Focus your mindfulness upon your heart.

Listen to the steady beat, and feel the weight of your own humanity.

We all listen to the same beat – we all contain the same heart.

Inhale for one, two, three, four, and picture a vase filled with flowers –

But empty of water.

Inhale for one, two, three, four, and exhale, for one, two, three, four.

The empty space at the bottom of the vase calls to you –

But what can you do?

Inhale for one, two, three, four,

And exhale for one, two, three, and four.

You have something to pour.

Return your focus to your chest.

You have love there.

Love to give.

Every slow inhale of breath, the picture that vase with a thin pool of water.

Breathe in for one, two, three, four,

And out, for one, two, three, and four.

Each petal moves, there is water there.

You cannot receive love if you are incapable of giving.

Inhale for one, two, three, four,

And exhale for one, two, three, and four.

Each flower, thirst, feel your compassion
– learn to give so that you may receive.

Learn to give so that you may receive.

Inhale for one, two, three, four, and give your love away.

Exhale one, two, three, and four - and watch the flowers in your vase.

As you breathe, you give, and you learn to love.

No closed heart can receive emotion.

Inhale for one, two, three, four,

And exhale for one, two, three, and four.

Make a promise to yourself, like each returning breath –

Love given is love returned.

Love given is love returned.

Love given is love returned.

Inhale for one, two, three, four,

And exhale for one, two, three, and four.

You are a vessel and a traveler, a being and a spirit.

But love is both physical and spiritual.

One brings the other, and the other brings one.

Spiritual love breads physical love, and physical love breads spiritual love.

You are a pattern, a circle, a cycle.

Your love comes from your heart – within – and returns, to heal you, also within.

Inhale for one, two, three, four,

And exhale for one, two, three, and four.

Body and spirit, mind and matter. Love is both.

Give yourself permission to give your love away –

Only once you've done so will love to return your way.

As you begin to slowly surface, inhale for one, two, three,

And exhale for one, two, and three.

Allow your palms to close, slowly.

Body and spirit, mind and matter. Love is both.

And you are love.

Self-Compassion "Break" Meditation

Forgiveness Guided Self-Healing

As you settle into your practice, find a comfortable position.

Give yourself permission to slow down.

Forgiveness does not come easy on our own hearts –

Extend yourself the same courtesy you do to others.

We are gentle to our surroundings and gentle to our families.

We love others, animals, and the planet – but we fail to love ourselves.

Let your eyes fall however they like; keep your palms open, no matter your stance.

Invite the universe into your heart. Leave your personal space open for positivity.

Slowly, inhale through your nose, for one, two, three, four.

Exhale, slowly, through your mouth, one, two, three, and four.

Focus your mindfulness as you breathe, for one, two, three, four,

Find the compassion your mindfulness inspires –

Compassion for yourself will heal old wounds.

A centered being cannot be at odds within itself.

A mindful life must mind itself.

Inhale slowly, for one, two, three, four,

And exhale, one, two, three, and four.

If you come to your practice with guilt today, find it and hold it in your mind.

If you come to your practice with anger today, find it and hold it in your mind.

If you come to your practice with insecurity today, find it and hold it in your mind.

We, like the world, have many sides, many faces, and many hides.

You are not defined by a single one – all are many, but in love, we are one.

Inhale through your nose for one, two, three, four,

And release through your mouth, one, two, three, and four.

A body divided cannot find its center.

You must unite yourself with love.

Begin by extending yourself compassion.

Then, extend yourself protection.

You are safe to forgive – and you are not your mistakes.

Inhale deeply through your nose, one, two, three, four,

Focusing on the pain that you are holding in your mind.

Exhale for one, two, three, and four –

Cruelty towards ourselves hurts twice as much as others.

You are not your greatest critic; do not harm that which keeps you alive.

Even when you err, your mind, body, and spirit are precious.

Growth is learning, growth is recovery;
And forgiveness fuels that growth.
Do not let guilt make your spirit heavy.
Do not let anger make your spirit spiteful.
Do not let insecurity diminish your light.
You are powerful and capable of change.
Breathe in through your nose for one, two, three, four,
And out through your mouth – not slowly this time. Fast, hard, all in one gust.
Aggressive, like the wind – a purification.
HUUUUUUUUHHHHHH.
Guilt, anger, insecurity, pain –
Blow them out, with each exhales.
Hard and fast, let your mouth make a sound.
Give yourself permission to expel negative energy.
Give yourself permission to make noise –
Push and push until your pain is gone.
Only peace will soon remain.

Inhale for one, two, three, and four –
And blow OUT – hard – all in one breath.
Let it all go.
Push it all out.
Your mistakes do no good trapped inside where they can hurt you.

Inhale for one, two, three, and four –
And blow – OUT. Your pain is the past.
Inhale, for one, two, three, and four –
And blow – OUT. Your pain is the past.
Inhale for one, two, three, and four –
And blow – OUT. Your pain is the past.
Forgive yourself.

Inhale your pain, breathe in your hurt.
Expel compassion – be kind to your heart.
Inhale for one, two, three, and four –
And be gentle to your exhale – one, two, three, four.

You are forgiven now. Your mind is clear, your body is purged.

Your blood runs compassion.

There is love for yourself here, and in love for yourself, there is healing.

Let go of your guilt. Let go of your anger. Let go of your insecurities.

You are forgiven. You are mindful and compassionate.

You are a centered being.

Inhale your hard work for one, two, three, four,

And exhale your peace – one, two, three, four.

Inhale your past – one, two, three, four,

And exhale your peace – one, two, three, four.

Inhale your pain – one, two, three, four,

And exhale self- love – one, two, three, four.

Let forgiveness return your soul to center.

Move forward – and treat yourself with care.

Universal Compassion Meditation

Vipassana Meditation

One of the most ancient forms of Buddhist meditation involving only the recognition of the sense, Vipassana meditation is the building block for modern emotional control. Vipassana meditation seeks to relax your mind and focus only on the rising and falling of your natural body processes (i.e., your natural breathing). However, when you practice Vipassana, you want to make special note of the sensations you experience while you practice. For this style of meditation for guided self-healing, you'll want to sit somewhere quiet, either in nature or near nature, in a comfortable enough position that you won't have to move for a long while.

Come to your natural breath with respect and admiration.

Breathing is part of your life force – do not force what is natural.

Allow yourself to recline, comfortable, safe, and steady.

With your palms open to the sky and universe, close your eyes.

Breathe in for four counts – one, two, three, four,

And out for four counts – one, two, three, four.

Clear your mind. You want to purge your thoughts, slow your mind.

It is time for quiet.

It is time now for only your senses.

You are in communion with your existence – nature, earth, body, breath.

One.

As you breathe, think only of that.

Breathing.

You are breathing.

Do not allow your thoughts to intrude upon this space.
Your mind should be clear, clean, and pure.
Only breathing.
You are only breathing.
If your mind begins to wonder,
You are only thinking.
If you find yourself focused on your physical being,
You are only Feeling.
You are a body filled with sensation –
But you are also a body overwhelmed by it.
Inhale for one, two, three, four,
And exhale for one, two, three, and four.
Do not allow your complicated existence to intrude upon your silence.
Here, you are alone with only your feelings.
They are all that matter.
Breathing.
You are only breathing.
Inhale for one, two, three, four,

And exhale for one, two, three, and four.
A sound might pass – but you cannot help Hearing.
Acknowledge the action – I am hearing.
But do not allow it to stay past its welcome.
You are not Hearing or Smelling, You are not thinking.
A scent may pass – but don't stall while you're Smelling.
You are not Smelling –
You are only breathing.
Note, and then erase.
Breathing.
Breathing.
You are only breathing.
Inhale for one, two, three, four,
And exhale for one, two, three, and four.
Your thoughts do not belong here –
Your feelings do not belong here –
Your smells do not belong here –
Your sounds do not belong here –
Here is only peace.

Here is the rest.
Here is quiet.
Here, you breathe.
In – one, two, three, four.
Out – one, two, three, four.
The simplest form of focus, here, in only your breath, upon only your life.
You need nothing but air.
You need nothing but breath.
Quiet your mind – You are only breathing.

Anxiety Meditation

Many individuals who struggle with anxiety or depression have individualized scripts and routines that help them manage their symptoms. However, there are a few general concepts and meditative techniques that can help almost anyone meditate for their anxiety. While these scripts might not be fool-proof for every form of anxiety or anxiety disorder, any sort of meditation or mindfulness is scientifically proven to help manage them. Let's get started.

General Self-Healing Script for On-The-Spot Anxiety Relief

Find a comfortable space where you feel most safe.

Center your mindful brain upon your breath.

Let your lungs fill with air – one, two, three, four.

Air brings your body life, and your breath keeps you safe.

Here and now, you are real. Focus only on what is real.

The present is now – and it safe for you here.

Exhale for one, two, three, and four.

Look around you. What do you see?

Name four things that you can find.

Inhale and count – one, two, three, four.

Each item, a breath. Feel your feelings de-escalate.

Exhale for one, two, three, and four.

Listen to your surroundings. What do you hear?

Name four sounds that you hear in your ears,

Breathe them in for one, two, three, and four.

And out, for one, two, three, and four.

Your surroundings help you ground your spirit. Hold yourself to the Earth.

You are present. Wherever you are where you can be. You can only control yourself.

Take charge of your breath – inhale for one, two, three, four, and hold –

Two, three, four - exhale, and feel your influence over your breath.

You are in control. Not your anxiety.

You are in control. Not your anxiety. You are grounded and ruled by your mindfulness.

Remind yourself.

Inhale for one, two, three, four – and relish in your ability to rest, here, where you have power.

No matter what happens around you,

Stress, tension, fear, pain – you, your mind, and your breath are safe.

These are yours. Find comfort in your body.

Find comfort in your center.

Breathe in for one, two, three, and four –
And out – one, two, three, and four.
Expel your fear. You have control.
Your center grounds you.
Your breath gives your life.
All you need is you.

Guided Anxiety Meditation for Active Brains

As you come to your practice today, keep a slow, steady pace –

You are here to calm, here to rest, and here to slow down.

Find a restful position with your palms gently open.

Inhale for four counts – one, two, three, four,

And out for four counts – one, two, three, four.

Focus on your chest, the rising and falling of your natural breath.

Your mind and anxiety pull you off center, further from stability.

But you are strong – you can pull them back.

Inhale for one, two, three, four,

And exhale for one, two, three, and four.

Focus on your brain now, your thoughts, your words, and your constant stream of sounds.

You are thinking, thinking, but you seek only quiet.

Return to your breath.

Inhale for one, two, three, four,

And exhale, for one, two, three, four.

As you breathe, focus your thoughts on a single chant.

One word, strong, powerful.

Mindful.

Clear.

Breathing.

Breathing.

Breathing.

Inhale for one, two, three, four,

And exhale for one, two, three, and four.

Allow your body to chant, consistent, focused – mindful.

Breathing.

You are breathing.

Feel your body revel in breath and silence.

If your mind begins to stray – bring it back to the center.

Breathing. Chant. You are breathing. Thinking comes later.

For now, only breathing.

Inhale for one, two, three, four,

And exhale for one, two, three, and four.

Let the rise and fall of your chest relax your muscles.

Your mind can rest – it is okay to rest.

Thinking becomes Worrying,

Breathing is living.

Inhale for one, two, three, four,

And exhale for one, two, three, and four.

Your mind is not in control while your breath rules your focus.

Your mind is not in control. Your breath rules your focus.

Breathing.

Breathing.

The activity has a place, but only with your permission.

Your mind is under your domain.

You have absolute control.

You are breathing.

There is no room for thinking.

Breathing.

Breathing.

Inhale for one, two, three, four,

And exhale for one, two, three, and four.

Inhale for one, two, three, four,

And exhale for one, two, three, and four.

Breathing.

You are breathing.

There is no room for anxious thoughts on a breath of air.

Let your mind calm. Every exhale, your mind quiets.

Inhale for one, two, three, four,

And exhale, silence – one, two, three, four.

Inhale – one, two, three, four,

And exhale, silence – one, two, three, four.

Breathing only.

Breathing only.

Inhale – one, two, three, four,

And exhale, silence – one, two, three, four.

Come to rest in silence.

Allow your peace to quiet.

You are calm. You are breathing.

Your mind is silent.

Your breath is strong.

Inhale –one, two, three, four,

And exhale one, two, three, and four.

You are calm. Your mind rests.

Finally, if you found this book useful in any way, a review on Amazon is always appreciated!

www.ingramcontent.com/pod-product-compliance
Lightning Source LLC
Chambersburg PA
CBHW060358080526
44583CB00012B/366